PLANETS IN OUR SOLAR SYSTEM

Learn About MARS!

BY NATALIE HUMPHREY

Enslow PUBLISHING

DISCOVER!

Please visit our website, www.enslow.com. For a free color catalog of all our high-quality books, call toll free 1-800-398-2504 or fax 1-877-980-4454.

Cataloging-in-Publication Data

Names: Humphrey, Natalie.
Title: Learn about Mars! / Natalie Humphrey.
Description: New York : Enslow Publishing, 2024. | Series: Planets in our solar system | Includes index.
Identifiers: ISBN 9781978533554 (pbk.) | ISBN 9781978533561 (library bound) | ISBN 9781978533578 (ebook)
Subjects: LCSH: Mars (Planet)–Juvenile literature.
Classification: LCC QB641.H857 2024 | DDC 523.43–dc23

Portions of this work were originally authored by Daisy Allyn and published as *Mars: The Red Planet.* All new material in this edition authored by Natalie Humphrey.

Published in 2024 by
Enslow Publishing
2544 Clinton Street
Buffalo, NY 14224

Designer: Andrea Davison-Bartolotta
Editor: Natalie Humphrey

Photo credits: Cover (Mars), pp. 1 (Mars), 15 Pike-28/Shutterstock.com; cover (top), p. 1 (top), series art (backgrounds) Jurik Peter/Shutterstock.com; series art (lens flare) andruxevich/Shutterstock.com; p. 4 Natee Jitthammachai/Shutterstock.com; pp. 5, 17 Vadim Sadovski/Shutterstock.com; p. 7 Artins/Shutterstock.com; p. 9 Pavel Gabzdyl/Shutterstock.com; p. 11 (inset) Dotted Yeti/Shutterstock.com; p. 11 (main) NASA/JPL-Caltech/Cornell/NMMNH; p. NASA/JPL/University of Arizona; p. 19 (both) NASA/JPL-Caltech/MSSS; p. 21 courtesy of NASA.

Printed in the United States of America

CPSIA compliance information: Batch #CS24ENS: For further information contact Enslow Publishing, at 1-800-398-2504.

CONTENTS

Boldface words appear in Words to Know.

Mysterious MARS

The fourth planet in our **solar system**, Mars is known as the "red planet." Why? Because it looks red from Earth! But that's not the only shocking thing about Earth's neighbor. Scientists believe that a long time ago, Mars may have had water!

Mars is about 142 million miles (230 million km) from the sun.

Time on MARS

It takes a long time for Mars to **orbit** the sun. One year on Mars takes around 687 days on Earth! But one day on Mars is very close to a day on Earth. It takes around 24 hours and 40 minutes for Mars to spin completely.

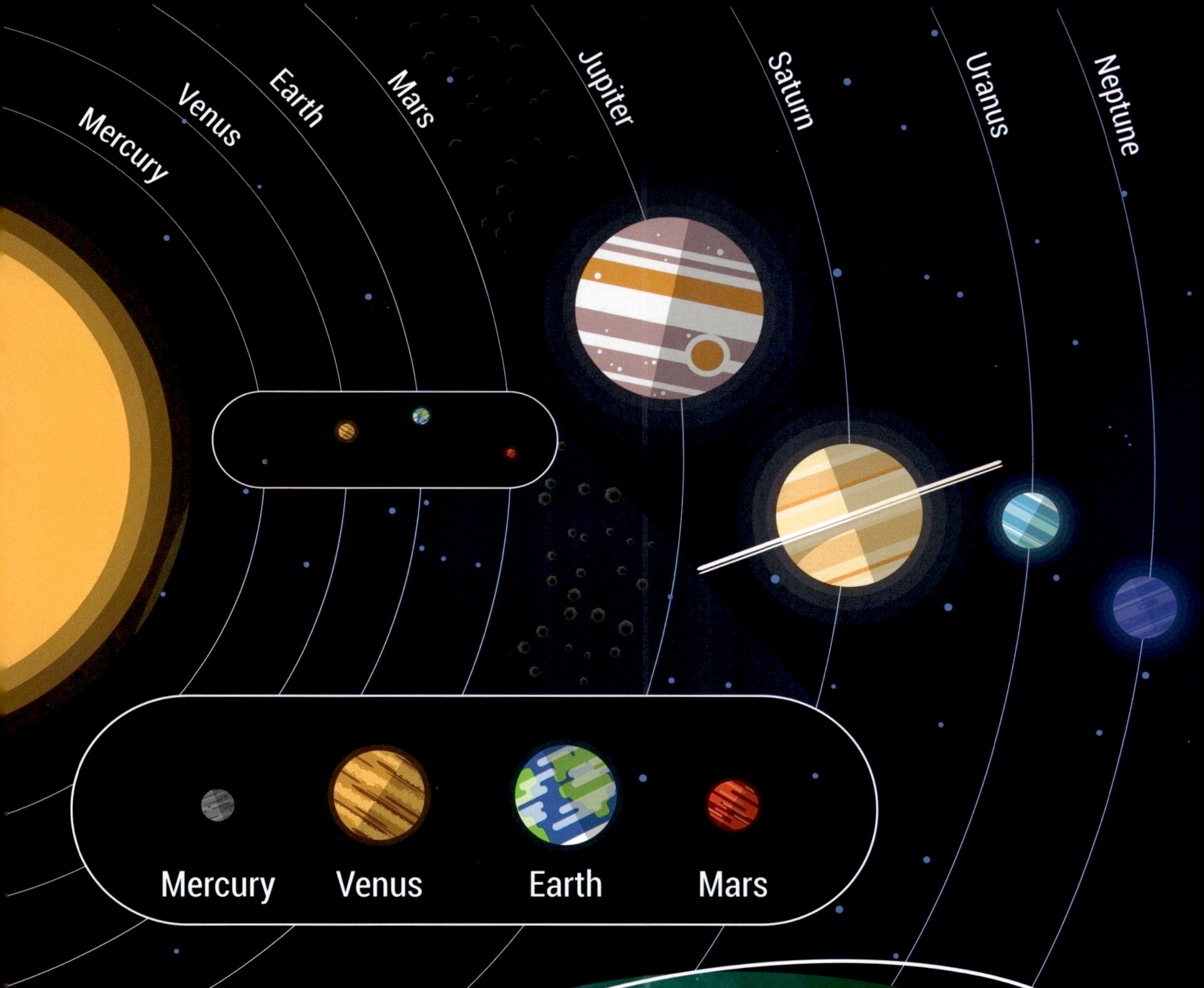

Scientists believe Mars is the planet that is the most similar to Earth.

Mars' MOONS

There are two moons orbiting Mars. They are called Phobos (FOH-bohs) and Deimos (DAY-mohs). These two moons aren't much like Earth's moon. They are much smaller and are not round. Phobos and Deimos orbit closer to Mars than any other planet's moon.

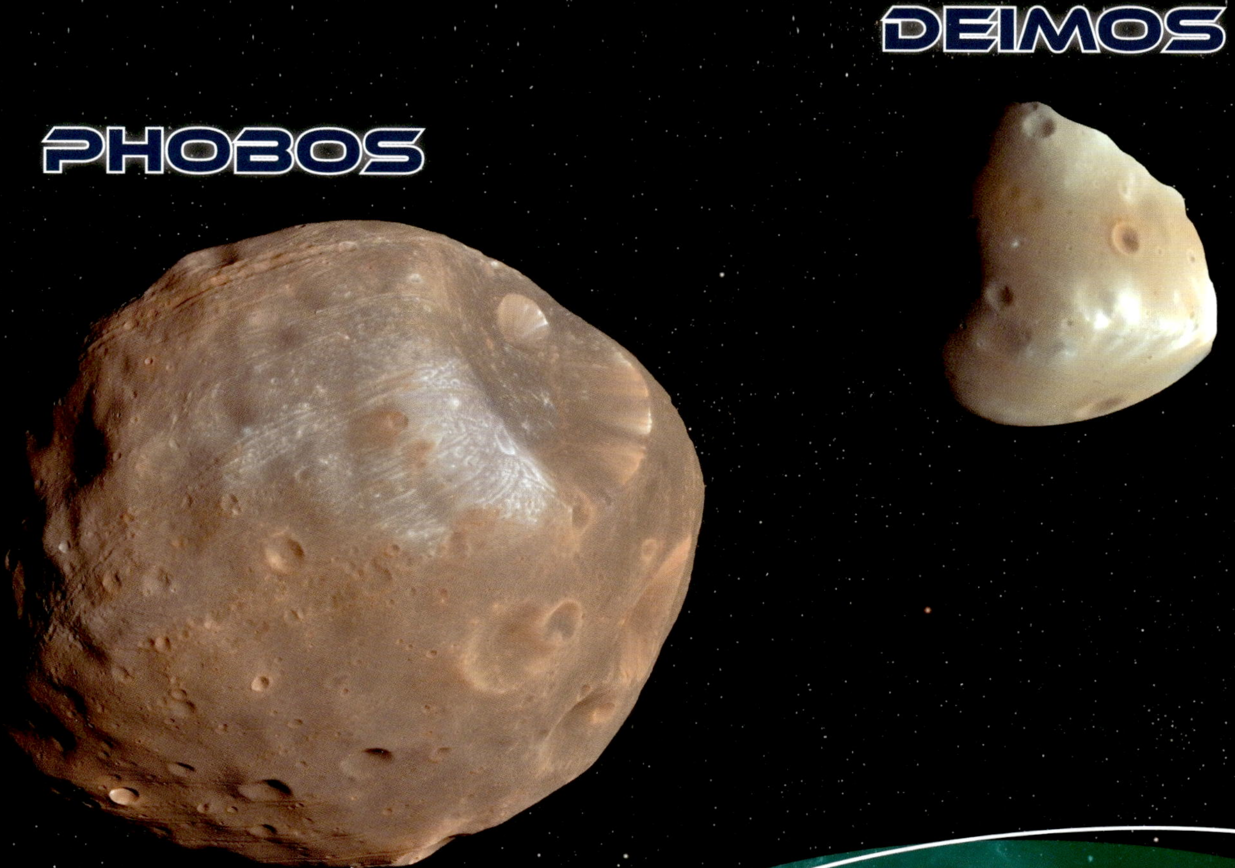

Phobos orbits Mars three times each day.

Red DESERT

The surface of Mars looks like a red desert with lots of **canyons** and **volcanoes**. The sand on Mars is made out of mostly iron. That makes it look red. Sometimes, Mars has dust storms that can cover the whole planet!

The highest mountain and volcano on Mars is Olympus Mons. It is much taller than Mount Everest.

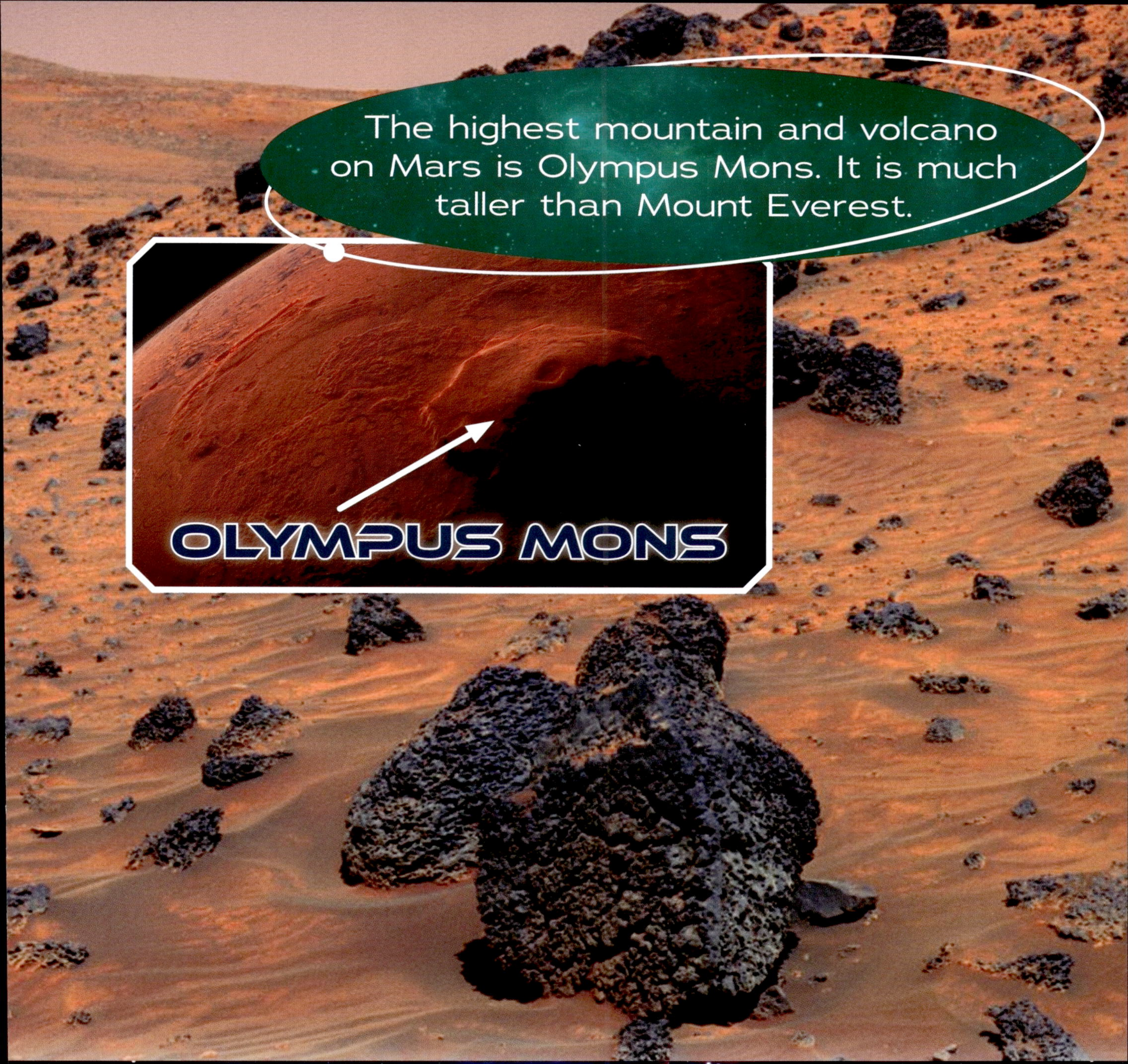

Freezing AT NIGHT

Mars' **atmosphere** is very thin. Because of this, Mars can't trap heat from the sun! During the day, Mars can be around 70°F (21°C). At night, though, Mars gets very cold. It can be as cold as –200°F (–129°C)!

Even though it doesn't rain on Mars, scientists have seen frost on the ground.

Ancient RIVERS

Just like Earth's **poles**, Mars' poles are covered with ice! This makes scientists believe that Mars might have been covered with water. There is also some possible proof of **erosion** that scientists believe may have been caused by water that isn't there anymore.

Scientists believe there could still be water deep underground on Mars.

Layers of MARS

Mars has many layers just like Earth. The first rocky layer we can see is called the crust. Under the crust, Mars has another rocky layer called the mantle. Inside the mantle is Mars' core. The core is made of **dense** metal.

Mars is about half the size of planet Earth.

Life on MARS

Could there be life on Mars? Some scientists believe there used to be! To look at the surface up close, NASA created special robots called rovers. These rovers explore the surface of Mars and send back pictures and **information**.

There are two NASA rovers currently running on Mars: Perseverance and Curiosity.

In 2017, NASA announced Project Artemis. This **mission** would first set up a base on the moon. Then, after the base is up and running, scientists will start planning their mission to Mars! What do you think they'll find there?

If everything goes right, the first step to sending people to Mars could be landing two **astronauts** on the moon in 2025!

WORDS TO KNOW

astronaut: Someone who works or lives in space.

atmosphere: The mixture of gases that surround a planet.

canyon: A deep valley with steep sides.

dense: Packed very closely together.

erosion: The act of wearing away by water, wind, or ice.

information: Knowledge obtained from study or observation.

mission: A task or job a group must perform.

orbit: To travel in a circle or oval around something.

pole: Either point of the imagined line around which a planet turns.

solar system: The sun and all the space objects that orbit it, including the planets and their moons.

volcano: An opening in a planet's surface through which hot, liquid rock sometimes flows.

FOR MORE INFORMATION

BOOKS

Leed, Percy. *Mars: A First Look*. Minneapolis, MN: Lerner Publications, 2023.

Storm, Marysa. *Mars*. Mankato, MN: Black Rabbit Books, 2023.

WEBSITES

NASA Space Place
spaceplace.nasa.gov/all-about-mars/en/
Learn fun facts, check out cool photos, and more from NASA!

National Geographic Kids
kids.nationalgeographic.com/space/article/mission-to-mars
Find photos, videos, and more information about Mars here!

Publisher's note to educators and parents: Our editors have carefully reviewed these websites to ensure that they are suitable for students. Many websites change frequently, however, and we cannot guarantee that a site's future contents will continue to meet our high standards of quality and educational value. Be advised that students should be closely supervised whenever they access the internet.

INDEX